FANTASY CREATURES

Troll

WRITTEN BY MICHAEL TEITELBAUM • ILLUSTRATED BY RON ZALME

A Creative Media Applications Production

Art Direction by Fabia Wargin Design

ISBN 0-8167-4516-1

10 9 8 7 6 5 4 3 2 1

S tep into an amazing world filled with witches, goblins, elves, and more—a world that YOU create! Battle fierce dragons, hairy trolls, and a people-eating Cyclops. Seek the aid of a good wizard, a fairy princess, or a unicorn. What happens in this world is up to you!

In this book, you will learn how to draw 18 different fantasy creatures—some good, some evil, some possessing fantastic powers. You will also learn how to draw backgrounds for your characters to appear in and props for them to use in the stories you make up.

Follow the simple, step-by-step instructions, and soon you'll be drawing your own elves, ogres, and other fantasy creatures. Practice is the key to being a good artist, so work on each character again and again.

Materials

- **medium pencil**
- **fine- to medium-point black felt-tip marker**
- **eraser**
- **8 1/2" x 11" (21.5 cm x 28 cm) sheets of white paper**
- **tracing paper**

Be patient, take your time, and let the adventure begin!

Here are the basic shapes you can use to draw everything in this book.

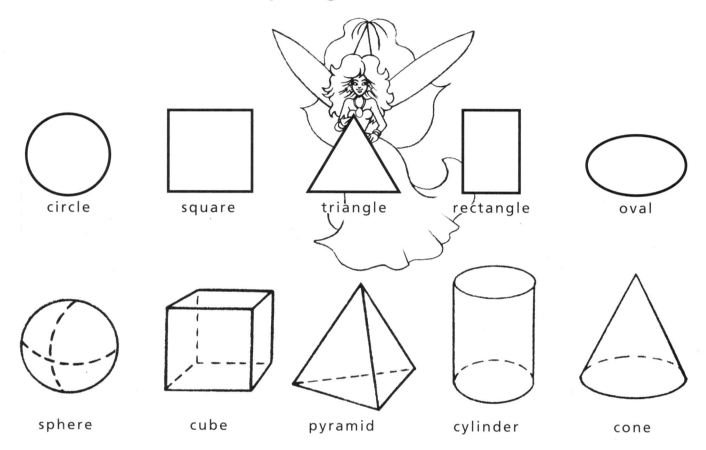

circle square triangle rectangle oval

sphere cube pyramid cylinder cone

Everything you draw with your pencil is a two-dimensional flat shape, like the five basic shapes at the top of this page. However, using techniques you'll learn in this book, you can create the illusion of an actual three-dimensional object in your drawings. Look at the circle above. It is round and two-dimensional. Now pick up a ball. The ball is also round, but it is three-dimensional, an actual object. The trick to drawing believable characters is to create the illusion on paper that what you are drawing is three-dimensional (like the ball), even though it is really only two-dimensional (like the circle). Look at the drawing of the sphere shown in the second row. The sphere is the three-dimensional "partner" to the circle. You can see that just by adding the two crisscrossing dotted lines to the drawing of the circle, you can create the illusion of the three-dimensional sphere. The same can be done with each of the shapes shown on this page. Practice drawing the two-dimensional shapes, then work on the 3-D shapes like the cube, pyramid, etc. After you've practiced for a while, you'll be ready to start drawing your first fantasy creature!

Elf

Elves are fun-loving little beings who possess many powers. Most elves are good, but some are devilish. Elves live in woods and meadows, and on hills. They can be helpful to people, but sometimes they like to play harmless tricks, like stealing something, then returning it. If you can make a friend of an elf, you have a loyal pal for life.

❶

Begin with a pencil. When you are done, you'll erase the extra pencil lines and darken the important character lines. Start by drawing a circle for the head. Next add vertical and horizontal "crosshairs." This will help you map out where the facial features will go, and which way the character is facing. You will use these on every character in the book. Then add the circles, squares, and other shapes, as shown.

❷

Create a shape, as shown, to indicate his hair. Draw two more triangles to complete the arms, then add the shapes shown for the shirt, belt, and boots.

❸

Use the crosshairs to line up the eyes, nose, and mouth, as shown. Now add details for the clothes, belt, boots, hair, hat, and feather. Be creative. Your drawing doesn't have to look exactly like the one in the book!

❹

Look for all the final details shown in this drawing, such as ears, eyebrows, buttons, and laces. Add them to your drawing. Then make up a few details of your own and put them in, too. Now darken the important lines in your drawing and erase the extra pencil lines. Congratulations! You've just completed your first fantasy creature.

Fairy Princess

airy princesses are tiny, magical creatures who fly through the air on delicate wings and can make themselves invisible. Fairy princesses can be mischievous, but they are always kind and helpful to humans. They give toys to children, and their magic can break spells cast by witches.

1 Remember to always begin drawing lightly with a pencil. This time start out with an oval for the head. Again, draw the crosshairs. Add the triangles and circles, as shown. Next add the fairy wings. These are ovals with pointy ends.

2 Now add the facial features, using your crosshairs as guidelines, and outline her arms and hands. Then put in the hair, veil, and gown hem, as shown.

3 Add more detail to the hair, veil, and gown. Make up your own hair and gown style, or follow the lines shown here. Next, draw her hands, then give her bracelets and star-shaped earrings.

4 Touch up the details, then erase extra pencil lines. To complete the Fairy Princess, put a pattern onto her gown: flowers, stars, jewels, or whatever you like!

Faun

These cheerful woodland spirits live deep in the forest. Fauns have human heads with small horns and pointed ears. They have the tail, legs, and hooves of a goat. These magical creatures love to dance and play beautiful music on their flutes.

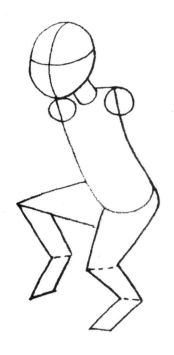

 Start with the head shape and crosshairs. Then add the long body shape and shoulders. The legs bend at some unusual angles, so we've added some dotted lines to help you draw the shapes.

 Add the facial features, horns, arms, tail, and hooves. To make the Faun's flute, draw a square on top of his hands and a triangle below, as shown.

 Finish the face. He is shown here with his eyes closed, but you can add pupils to give him opened eyes if you like. Add jagged lines along his edges to give him fur, and details to his hands, hooves, and flute.

 Draw hair on his head, and finish up the fur details. A black shadow on his neck helps to give a three-dimensional look to his head. Erase extra pencil lines, and your Faun is ready to dance!

Good Wizard

Wizards are the wisest of all magical creatures. Good wizards use their wisdom and magical powers to teach, spread knowledge, and bring happiness. They cast spells that protect weaker creatures from the evil in the world. Good wizards give advice to help people, and they use their magic to battle evil wizards and evil dragons.

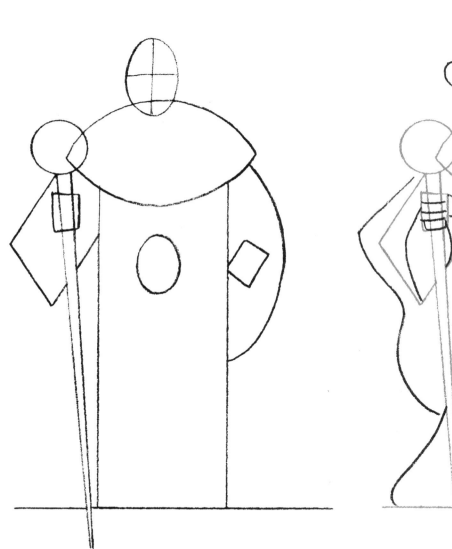

1 The Good Wizard is made up of some unusual shapes, but look for the more simple shapes we've used within the unusual ones. The body is made up of a football shape resting on top of a rectangle. Outline his head, arms, and staff (his magic wand), as shown.

2 Add the hat, beard, nose, and hands, and draw some lines to show where the hair will go. Outline his robe. His cape is being blown by the wind so you can be creative with its exact shape

3 Continue by drawing the hatband and amulet (the magical piece of jewelry around his neck). Add details to his face, cape, and staff. Change the straight lines of the hair and beard into curls to make them seem more lifelike.

4 Complete your figure by drawing in the eyes, the folds in the robe, and the details in his magic amulet. His staff can end in a crystal ball, as shown, or a bolt of lightning, if you like. Try it both ways. Remember to use a marker to darken the lines you want to keep, then erase the pencil lines you don't need.

Dwarf

Dwarfs look like small humans with long gray beards and wrinkled, leathery skin. They are miners who live deep within mountain caves, and they have the power to turn invisible. Dwarfs love feasting and dancing. They are excellent smiths (forgers of metal), weavers of cloth, and bakers. Dwarfs can see into the future and give advice to people.

1 Start with the head and crosshairs as usual. The body is shaped like a kidney bean and the hands start off as circles. Outline the arms and legs, as shown.

2 The nose is a partial oval, and the sleeve cuffs are partial circles. Add a curved line to show where his beard will be. Now add the hat, ears, mouth, belt, and boots, as shown.

3 The eyes and eyebrows, mustache, fingers, and belt buckle come next. Add other details carefully, as shown, to give your drawing lots of character.

4 Change the straight lines of his eyebrows, hair, and beard to curls. Have fun with the beard and get as creative as you like. Blacken in his belt, and add the remaining details, as shown. Erase extra pencil lines, and your Dwarf is done.

Mermaid

Mermaids are magical half-women, half-fish who live in an undersea world of beauty and riches. They have the upper body, arms, and head of a woman, and the lower body and tail of a fish. Mermaids can take human form and come ashore for short periods of time. They cannot speak and usually bring bad luck to sailors, appearing when a storm or disaster is about to take place.

1 Start off with the head and body shapes. The arms are the toughest part of drawing the Mermaid.

Follow the lines, as shown, using the dotted lines to show where the elbows will go. These dotted lines will be erased at the end.

2 Begin the face next, then draw the hair. Outline her hands and tail.

3 Add pearls around her neck and wrists, and details to her face, hair, hands, and tail.

4 Finish up your Mermaid by drawing the details of her tail and scales. Don't forget to erase any extra pencil lines.

Unicorn

The enchanting unicorn is a magical creature that looks like a white horse but has one long horn growing from the middle of its forehead. The unicorn is a symbol of love and peace. Its horn can turn dirty water pure and can make poison harmless. Any person lucky enough to see a unicorn will receive years of good fortune.

1 If you have ever drawn a horse before, then drawing a Unicorn will be a snap. If not, don't worry. Like all of the creatures in this book, the Unicorn begins with basic shapes. Use circles, squares, and triangles to set up your horse, as shown.

2 Add the mane and tail, making up your own style or following the style shown here Draw in hooves and facial details

3 Place the horn on the Unicorn's head, add more facial details, and add more detail to the mane and tail. Draw some fur over the hooves.

4 Add "twists" to the horn to give it a spiral shape. Then add some shading to the legs, as shown, to indicate which legs are closer to you and which are farther away.

Finally, darken the important lines of your drawing, eras extra pencil lines, and your lucky Unicorn is comple

Centaur

This half-horse, half-human has the legs and body of a horse and the chest, arms, and head of a human. Centaurs live high in the tallest mountains. Some are wise and friendly, the companions of great Greek heroes. Others are wild and violent and are known for starting wars.

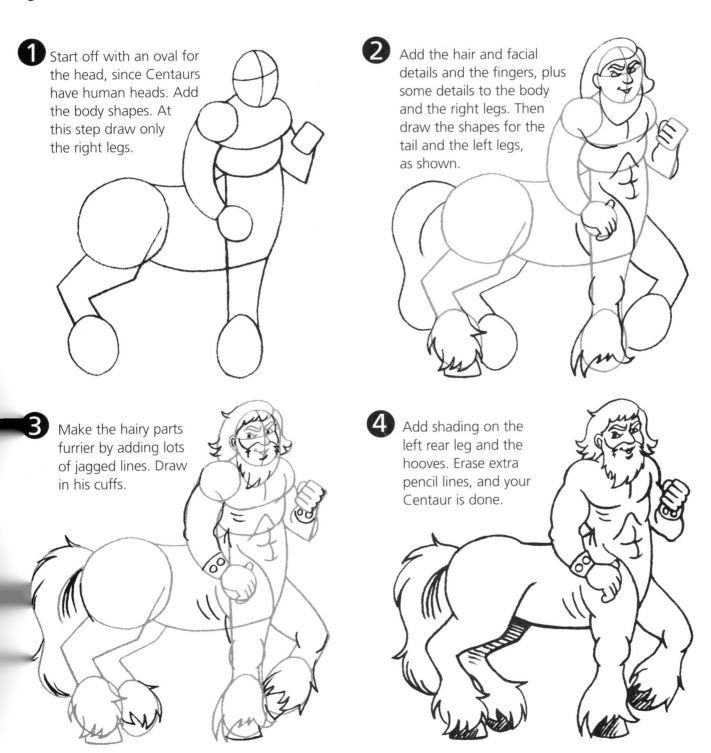

1 Start off with an oval for the head, since Centaurs have human heads. Add the body shapes. At this step draw only the right legs.

2 Add the hair and facial details and the fingers, plus some details to the body and the right legs. Then draw the shapes for the tail and the left legs, as shown.

3 Make the hairy parts furrier by adding lots of jagged lines. Draw in his cuffs.

4 Add shading on the left rear leg and the hooves. Erase extra pencil lines, and your Centaur is done.

Good Dragon

Good dragons have long, snakelike bodies and wings. They bring good luck wherever they fly. Evil dragons appear in the myths of most countries, but in China the dragon is a symbol of luck and is used during Chinese New Year's parades and celebrations.

1 The Good Dragon's head and body are made up of a series of linked circles and ovals. The starting wing shape looks like a half-circle or a big orange slice.

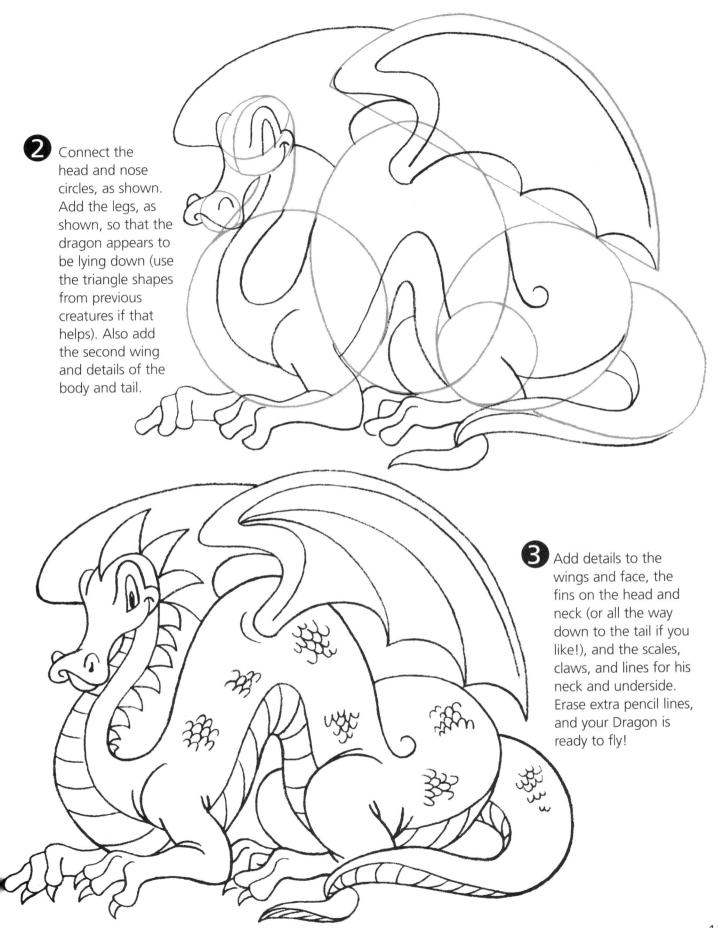

2 Connect the head and nose circles, as shown. Add the legs, as shown, so that the dragon appears to be lying down (use the triangle shapes from previous creatures if that helps). Also add the second wing and details of the body and tail.

3 Add details to the wings and face, the fins on the head and neck (or all the way down to the tail if you like!), and the scales, claws, and lines for his neck and underside. Erase extra pencil lines, and your Dragon is ready to fly!

Witch

itches have supernatural powers and practice magic. They are invulnerable (they cannot be hurt), have great strength, and can change their appearance to look like anyone. Witches can fly, turn invisible, and mix up magic potions in their cauldrons. These potions cause people to do whatever the witch desires.

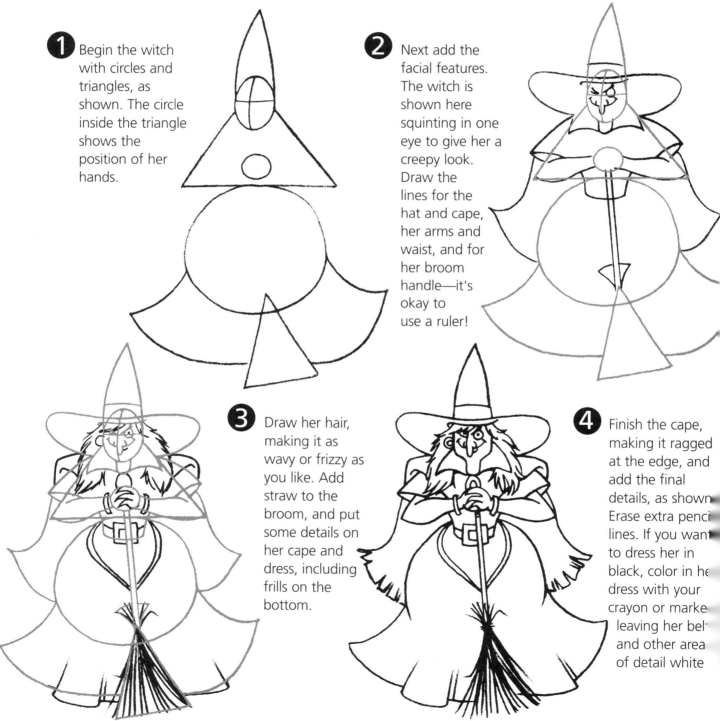

1 Begin the witch with circles and triangles, as shown. The circle inside the triangle shows the position of her hands.

2 Next add the facial features. The witch is shown here squinting in one eye to give her a creepy look. Draw the lines for the hat and cape, her arms and waist, and for her broom handle—it's okay to use a ruler!

3 Draw her hair, making it as wavy or frizzy as you like. Add straw to the broom, and put some details on her cape and dress, including frills on the bottom.

4 Finish the cape, making it ragged at the edge, and add the final details, as shown. Erase extra pencil lines. If you want to dress her in black, color in her dress with your crayon or marker, leaving her belt and other areas of detail white

Griffin

This powerful creature has the body of a lion and the head and wings of an eagle. Griffins can fly, and they live high in the mountains, where they guard their gold. Because their enemies are always trying to steal the griffins' gold, they have become great warriors, always ready to protect their treasure.

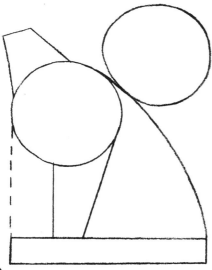

1 The Griffin's pose is unusual, so use a dotted vertical line to help line up the front of the creature as you draw its basic body shape.

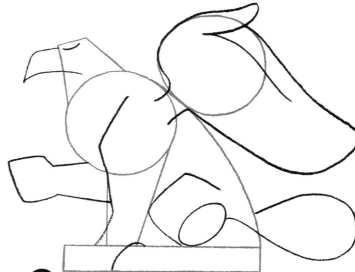

2 Work down from the highest circle to create one wing. The tail comes out like part of a figure eight. Next add the beak and the right front paw, and begin the two left legs.

3 Use curly lines to make the fur on its chest, elbows, and tail, giving the look of a lion's body. Add the second wing and detail to the first wing and body at this step.

4 Add feathers to the wings so that they look like those of an eagle. Black pads on the bottom of the raised paw add a touch of realism to the lion body. The serious eye and mouth and some shading on his tail complete this regal creature. Don't forget to erase extra pencil lines.

17

Goblin

Goblins are spirits that haunt houses. They can be helpful (they love to clean, for example), but they are also naughty and love pranks. Goblins try to frighten the people living in a house by knocking on walls, slamming doors, moving furniture in the night, breaking dishes, banging pots and pans, and even pulling the covers off while they sleep!

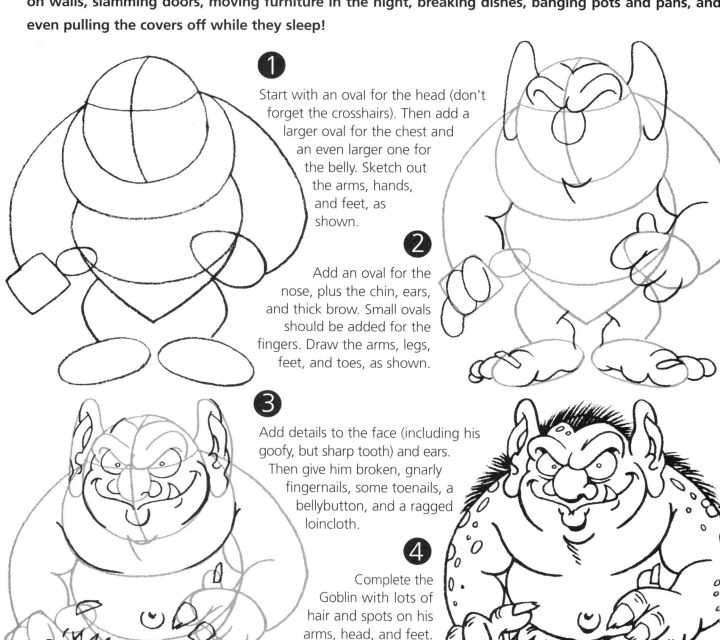

1 Start with an oval for the head (don't forget the crosshairs). Then add a larger oval for the chest and an even larger one for the belly. Sketch out the arms, hands, and feet, as shown.

2 Add an oval for the nose, plus the chin, ears, and thick brow. Small ovals should be added for the fingers. Draw the arms, legs, feet, and toes, as shown.

3 Add details to the face (including his goofy, but sharp tooth) and ears. Then give him broken, gnarly fingernails, some toenails, a bellybutton, and a ragged loincloth.

4 Complete the Goblin with lots of hair and spots on his arms, head, and feet. Shade in the loincloth so it looks like it is made from animal fur. Erase extra pencil lines, and your Goblin is ready for mischief!

Troll

Trolls are supernatural creatures with great strength and nasty tempers. They sometimes live in dark forests, castles, or mountain caves, where they guard treasures they have stolen. But most trolls live under bridges and attack anyone who tries to cross over the bridge. Trolls keep to the shadows, for if the sun ever shines on their faces, they burst apart, exploding into a million pieces.

1 Start with an oval for the Troll's head. His shoulders come next, extending down from where his ears will go. Notice the triangle shapes in his shoulders. Next comes a circle for his lower body, then the arms, legs, hands, and feet.

2 The little "hat" in this step is really there to show where his hair will go. Add facial features, then add the fingers, toes, and fur for the body.

3 Complete the face (notice the two teeth) and draw in his hair. Add some fur to his shoulders, chest, and the tops of his feet, and draw in fingernails and toenails.

4 Give your Troll some hair on his arms, and shade in his shins. This will help give him his primitive look. Erase any extra pencil lines, and you're done.

Evil Wizard

Evil wizards are very smart and are powerful magicians like their good cousins. But evil wizards use dark magic to harm and enslave weaker creatures. Their spells are used to conquer and destroy, and for personal gain. They battle the forces of good in the world, including good wizards and good dragons.

1 The upper part of the Evil Wizard's body is made from the simple shapes you have been using throughout the book. His body and robe will take a little practice. Work on the shape you see here, and be sure to make him tall compared with Dwarfs, Elves, and Trolls.

2 Sketch in the evil eyebrows and the long beard in this step. Outline his collar and sleeves, and draw his arms. The bottom of his robe should look like tree roots.

3 Add the two sides of his hat, which look like leaves, and start to fill in the facial features. Draw in his sleeves, which should have a shredded look, and add his collar and cape. Draw his fingers.

4 Change the straight lines of his eyebrows and beard to curls. Fill in the remaining details, as shown, including the dark areas of his fearsome face. Erase extra pencil lines. As with the witch, you can use black to color his robes. Red is also a good color to use for this evil creature.

Ogre

Ogres are hairy giants who like to eat people. Fortunately they are stupid, gullible, and easily frightened. An ogre can be scared off by the rustling of leaves in the woods, or easily tricked into diving into a lake to chase a reflection—ogres will believe anything you tell them.

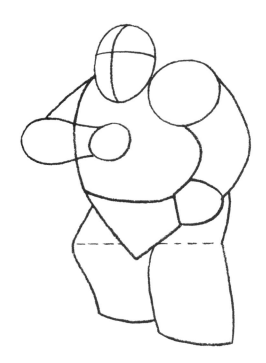

 Start with the shapes shown here, including the crosshairs on the face and the dotted lines to show where his knees will go.

 Start to fill in the facial details. His harness forms a big "X" on his chest. Add some fur to the bottom of his chest and outline his tail. Use curved lines for the tops of his boots to give the illusion that they go all the way around his legs.

 Continue adding details, including the two rhino horns on his shoulders, the circles on his harness, his studded wrist bands, and the leather straps that wrap around his boots. Use curly lines to show the fur on his head, arms, loincloth, and boots.

 The Ogre is a rough, nasty creature, so don't be afraid to give him a mean expression, complete with big teeth. Add the final details, as shown, then be sure to erase any extra pencil lines.

Cyclops

The Cyclops is a giant who has one eye in the middle of his forehead. This huge, uncivilized beast lives in a cave and eats humans! When it's not busy eating people, the Cyclops works as a shepherd, tending to flocks of sheep—a strange occupation for such a violent creature.

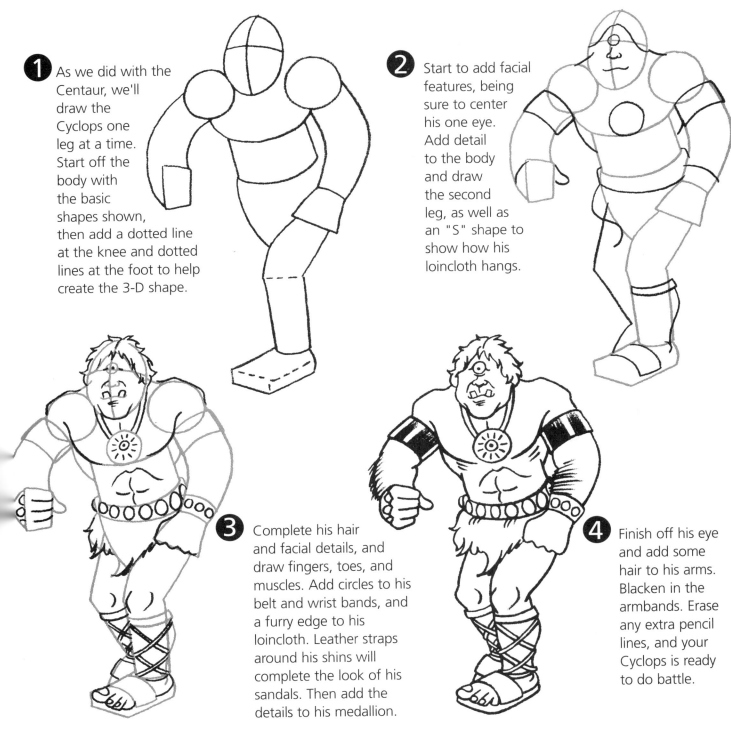

1 As we did with the Centaur, we'll draw the Cyclops one leg at a time. Start off the body with the basic shapes shown, then add a dotted line at the knee and dotted lines at the foot to help create the 3-D shape.

2 Start to add facial features, being sure to center his one eye. Add detail to the body and draw the second leg, as well as an "S" shape to show how his loincloth hangs.

3 Complete his hair and facial details, and draw fingers, toes, and muscles. Add circles to his belt and wrist bands, and a furry edge to his loincloth. Leather straps around his shins will complete the look of his sandals. Then add the details to his medallion.

4 Finish off his eye and add some hair to his arms. Blacken in the armbands. Erase any extra pencil lines, and your Cyclops is ready to do battle.

Medusa

Medusa was once a beautiful maiden, but the Greek goddess Athena envied her beauty and so turned her into a frightful monster. Medusa's lovely hair changed into writhing snakes, and her face is now so ugly that a glimpse of it will turn any living creature into stone!

1 Medusa's pose is different from that of our other creatures. Her head faces one way, and her body faces in the opposite direction. You can use a ruler to draw the straight lines of her gown. Be sure that she is very tall.

2 The snakes on Medusa's head are the hardest part of the character to draw. Practice drawing them and don't worry if they are not exactly like the snakes shown here. Get creative and make up your own evil-looking snakes. Add facial features, her gown, wings, and arms, one leg, and both feet at this step, too.

3 Keep adding snakes! Also, in this step, give her fangs, then earrings, an amulet, a waistband, and armbands—all the tools she needs to charm her victims and lure them to her! Draw her toes and begin to add detail to her wings.

4 Finish the details on the snakes' heads and Medusa's gown, wings, face, armbands, and ankle bracelet. Erase extra pencil lines. Legend says that her wings were golden, so if you like, color them with a gold crayon or marker.

Evil Dragon

These giant, flying, fire-breathing reptiles have huge wings and sharp claws. They announce their arrival with a roar that sounds like thunder. One evil dragon can destroy an entire town single-handedly. Evil dragons love to steal treasure, which they guard in their deep mountain caves.

1 This dragon may look complicated, but it's really just made up of shapes you have been using throughout the book. Start with the head and chest circles. Then add the kidney bean–shaped body (like you did with the Dwarf). The legs should be wide apart (like the Faun). Add the arms, and start to outline the tail and wings, as shown.

2 Be creative with the horns. They can bend in any direction you like. Start to draw his facial features. Add the claws and draw in the tail. Then draw the bottom edge of the wings with the curved shape shown so that they look like bat wings.

3 Add the teeth, some pointing up, some pointing down, and other facial details. Draw lines to show the ribs of his wings. Make the bottom edge of the wings ragged, and add a few rips in the wings to make it look as if he's been in many tough battles. Draw the lines on his chest and underside, add fins to the back of his neck, then put some scales on his body. Erase extra pencil lines, and your Dragon is ready to roar!

27

Scenery

After you've practiced drawing fantasy characters a few times, you'll be ready to place them into a scene. Here are a few settings you can use as backgrounds in which to place the characters you draw. Start off by tracing these backgrounds, then practice drawing them on your own. Place your fantasy characters into these scenes and make up your own stories.

Props

In any story you make up or picture you draw, your characters will need objects to hold and use. These are called props. Practice tracing, then drawing the props shown here. Then practice placing them into the hands (or claws) of the fantasy characters you draw, so they can use them in different situations. Finally, place your characters and props into the scenery and bring your stories to life!

FANTASY CREATURES